MUSIC IS MATH

AND HERE IT IS MADE EASY TO UNDERSTAND

AN EASY METHOD FOR READING
&
COUNTING MUSIC RHYTHM
PATTERNS
—FOR ALL AGES—

By Dr. Oliver W. Luck

About The Author

Music is Math

OLIVER W. LUCK

This is an easy method for reading and counting music rhythm patterns. Music is math and here it is made easy to understand. Dr. Oliver W. Luck is a composer arranger, conductor, and inventor. He is listed in "The Directory of Distinguished Americans", 1983 and also in "Personalities of the West and Midwest", 1983.

He attended Duquesne University, Carnegie Mellon University, and completed his undergraduate work and part of his graduate work at Michigan State University, where he also studied Music Therapy. He received his Masters degree at San Diego State University and his Ed.D at Pacific Western University.

Dr. Luck has taught music in the public schools from kindergarten through 12[th grade] including general music, band, orchestra, chorus, marching band, and jazz. He has also set up a music program for the Special Olympics. He was Director of Music at the V.A. Center in Dayton, Ohio for the federal government. Besides having performed with symphony orchestras and played for Broadway road shows including Captain Kangaroo, he has performed recording dates with Bing Crosby, Jack Jones, Connie Francis, and Petula Clark.

He was a member of the 657th Air Force band, the Duke Ellington, Louis Bellson, Cab Calloway and Buddy Webb bands and headed his own quintet. He has performed with Sammy Davis Jr. in the theater in the round and has performed throughout Europe with the King Solomon Burke orchestra and in San Diego with the Benny Hollman big band.

Order this book online at www.trafford.com
or email orders@trafford.com

Most Trafford titles are also available at major online book retailers.

Print information available on the last page.

ISBN: 978-1-4120-5912-1 (sc)
ISBN: 978-1-4122-0423-1 (e)

Trafford rev. 01/06/2022

Trafford PUBLISHING® www.trafford.com

North America & international
toll-free: 844-688-6899 (USA & Canada)
fax: 812 355 4082

Acknowledgements

To the many musicians I have had the opportunity to perform with and the fantastic teachers I have been blessed to have had the opportunity to be in their class, and to my friend and fellow musician who was really my greatest inspiration to play music the one and only Mr. Albert N. Aarons, Trumpeter extraordinaire. Special recognition to Bob and Reen Keller for the time and dedication spent in editing and putting this second edition together.   Dr. Oliver W. Luck

Jazz Times: Music is Math by Oliver W. Luck. "With compliments"— Stanley Dance, Book Editor.

"Oliver, this is a subject that I suspect my music teacher didn't quite completely cover. I'd be interested in one of your books. It's already helped me understand 6/8 time."   *J.Freeland*

Jazz Times: "Dr. Luck has found not only a good title for his book of music instruction for beginners, but also an excellent concept for the understanding of syncopation or time. Instead of introducing multiplication, as a theory involved in notation, he prefers to divide. His title, Music Is Math, is rightly subtitled, And Here It Is Made Easy to understand. Notes are sounded, counted and numbered, he explains. Rests are counted, but not numbered. In an example of how this works, he proposes dividing a circle, a pie, into halves, quarters, eights, sixteenths. When Illustrated with his large diagrams such notation becomes easily comprehensible. Quarter and eight note triplets are counted out as examples, and placed in context in meters involving 4/4,3/4,6/8,7/4,9/8,12/8 and 2/2.

In fewer than 24 pages of manuscript, this experienced, versatile and innovative educator demonstrates for people who love to play or sing, but were never taught how to count, a simple approach for reading rhythm patterns.

Besides teaching, the trombone-playing author has performed with symphony orchestras, Broadway road shows, the 657th Air Force band, and the Duke Ellington, Louie Bellson and Cab Calloway bands, and on records with Bing Crosby, Jack Jones, Connie Francis and Pettula Clark." — *Helen Oakley Dance*

TABLE OF CONTENTS

Title	**Page**

Music is Math

This easy method for reading and counting music rhythm patterns was written to help the many persons who love to play music or sing but were never taught how to count musically. This is one of the reasons so many instruments sit idle in a closet during and after graduation from high school and college. Here is a key I strongly suggest that you use to help you when you first begin using this counting concept.

A slash (/). The slash is used to determine if you have counted a measure or rhythm pattern correctly or how a music pattern should be played. Always place as many slashes above a measure as it would take to place as many of the smallest notes in the measure. If the measure would use 16 sixteenth notes in the measure then you would need sixteen slashes. (See example on page 10.) Put a line through each slash as each note or rest is counted in the measure.

Diagrams, pictures and examples are given to make each page easy to understand and each example easy to follow.

If each diagram and each example is completely understood, then each person should be able to number correctly all of the music problems at the end of the book. If there are some problems you have trouble with, go back and review that particular area. With the completion and understanding of this book, you can look forward to many years of musical enjoyment and happy days of sight reading music.

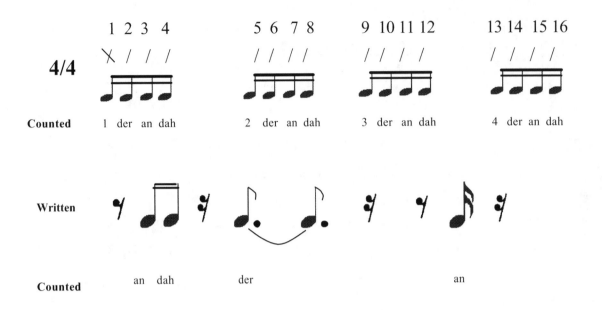

	1 2 3 4	5 6 7 8	9 10 11 12	13 14 15 16

4/4

Counted   1 der an dah   2 der an dah   3 der an dah   4 der an dah

Written

Counted   an dah   der   an

The note is only sounded within each measure. As you count each note or rest in the measure, cross off a slash above the note or rest. At the completion of each measure, each note and each rest should be accounted for. Remember to use as many slashes as there are the smallest note values in a measure.

Number of slashes in a measure

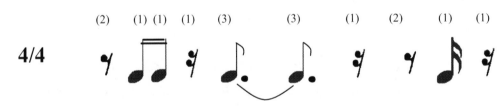

(2)   (1) (1)   (1)   (3)   (3)   (1)   (2)   (1)   (1)

4/4

Using the slash system you will be able to figure out how to play a rhythm pattern.

LET'S GET STARTED

NOTES ARE
> SOUNDED,
>> COUNTED, AND
>>> NUMBERED.

EXAMPLE:

RESTS
> ARE NOT
>> SOUNDED,
>>> BUT ARE COUNTED
>>>> THEREFORE, RESTS
>>>>> ARE NOT
>>>>>> NUMBERED

EXAMPLE:

EACH NOTE THAT IS WITHIN A MEASURE IS SOUNDED, SO IT MUST BE COUNTED. BEING THAT IT IS SOUNDED, IT IS NUMBERED.

EXAMPLE:

EACH REST THAT IS WITHIN A MEASURE IS NOT SOUNDED, BUT IT MUST BE COUNTED. BEING THAT IT IS NOT SOUNDED, IT IS NOT NUMBERED.

EXAMPLE:

MUSIC IS MATH, AND HERE IT IS MADE EASY TO UNDERSTAND. HERE IS A VERY BASIC CONCEPT:

AN APPLE PIE SELLS FOR ONE DOLLAR ($1.00)

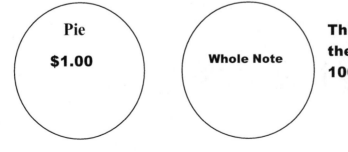

Pie

$1.00

Whole Note

This whole note equals the value of $1.00 or 100%

**CUT THE PIE IN HALF AND EACH HALF PIECE OF PIE COSTS 50¢.
THE TWO HALVES OF PIE EQUAL A WHOLE PIE, OR COST $1.00.**

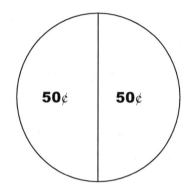

**CUT THE PIE INTO QUARTERS OR FOURTHS AND EACH PIECE OF PIE
COSTS 25¢, OR ONE FOURTH ¼ OF A DOLLAR,**

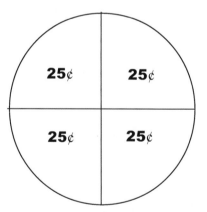

**AND IT TAKES FOUR QUARTER PIECES OF PIE TO EQUAL A
WHOLE PIE, AND TWO QUARTER PIECES OF PIE TO EQUAL A
HALF OF A PIE.**

CUT THE PIE INTO EIGHT, EQUAL PIECES OF PIE. EACH EIGHTH PIECE OF PIE WILL COST TWELVE AND ONE HALF CENTS (12½¢) AND IT WILL TAKE TWO EIGHTH PIECES OF PIE TO EQUAL ONE QUARTER PIECE OF PIE, FOUR EIGHTH PIECES OF PIE ARE EQUAL TO A HALF PIECE OF PIE. SIX EIGHTH PIECES OF PIE EQUAL THREE FOURTHS OF A PIE, AND EIGHT EQUAL PIECES OF PIE ARE EQUAL TO A WHOLE PIE.

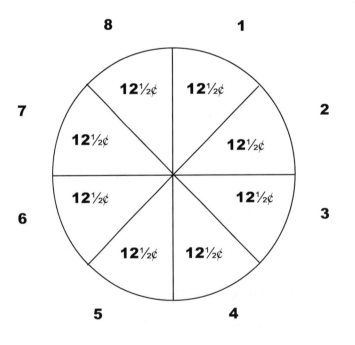

THIS EXAMPLE OF COUNTING THE NUMBER OF PIECES OF PIE TO EQUAL A WHOLE PIE IS EXACTLY THE SAME AS WHEN YOU COUNT NOTE VALUES IN MUSIC.

IT TAKES EIGHT EIGHTH NOTES TO EQUAL ONE WHOLE PIE OR ONE WHOLE NOTE.

Pie

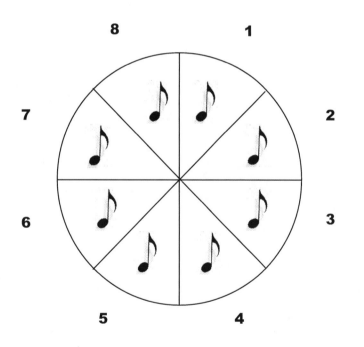

CUT THE PIE INTO SIXTEEN EQUAL PIECES. EACH SIXTEENTH
PIECE WILL COST SIX AND ONE-FOURTH CENTS (6¼¢). IT WILL
TAKE TWO SIXTEENTH PIECES TO EQUAL ONE EIGHTH PIECE OF
PIE, FOUR SIXTEENTH PIECES TO EQUAL ONE QUARTER PIECE OF
PIE. EIGHT SIXTEENTH PIECES OF PIE WILL EQUAL ONE HALF
PIECE OF PIE. TWELVE SIXTEENTH PIECES OF PIE WILL EQUAL
THREE-QUARTERS PIECES OF PIE, AND SIXTEEN SIXTEENTH PIECES
OF PIE WILL EQUAL A WHOLE PIE.

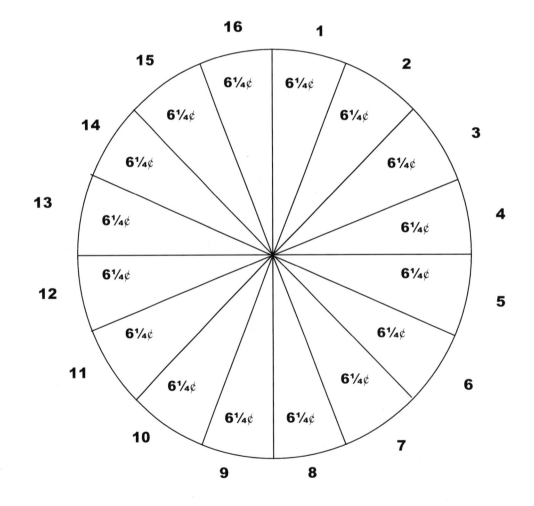

THIS EXAMPLE OF COUNTING THE NUMBER OF PIECES OF PIE TO EQUAL A WHOLE PIE IS EXACTLY THE SAME AS WHEN YOU COUNT NOTE VALUES IN MUSIC. IT TAKES SIXTEEN SIXTEENTH NOTES TO EQUAL ONE WHOLE PIE OR ONE WHOLE NOTE.

Pie

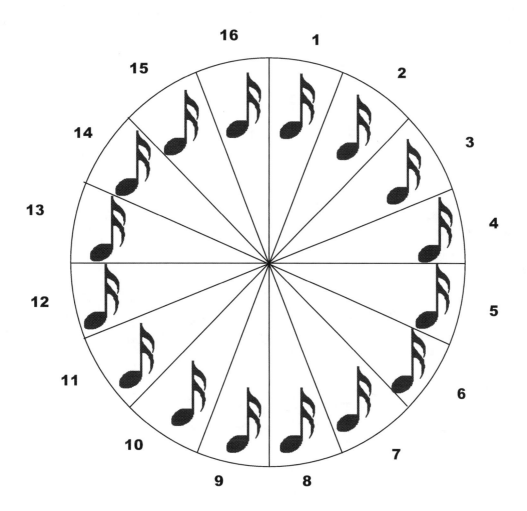

EXAMPLE OF NOTE VALUES

EXAMPLE:
AN APPLE PIE MAY BE—

EXAMPLE:
A NOTE'S VALUE MAY BE—
—

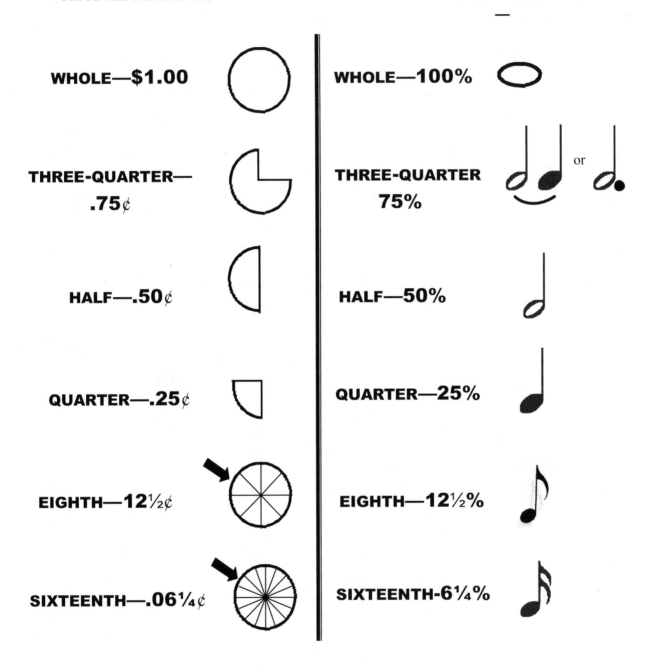

WHOLE—$1.00

WHOLE—100%

THREE-QUARTER—
.75¢

THREE-QUARTER
75%

HALF—.50¢

HALF—50%

QUARTER—.25¢

QUARTER—25%

EIGHTH—12½¢

EIGHTH—12½%

SIXTEENTH—.06¼¢

SIXTEENTH-6¼%

EXAMPLES OF DOT VALUES:

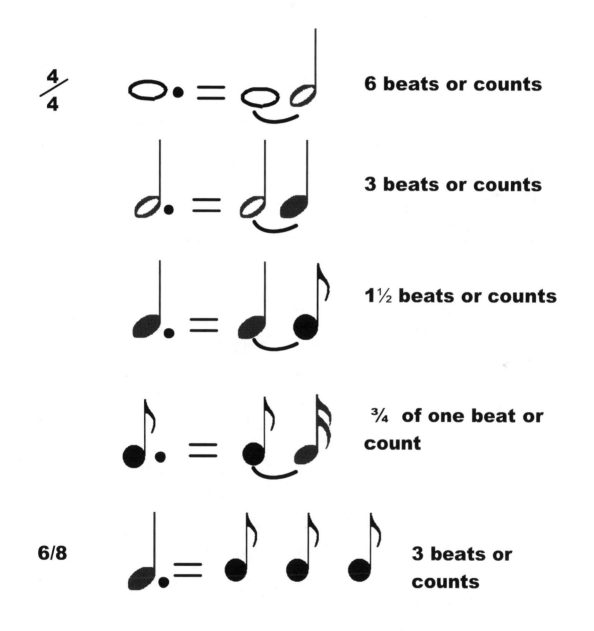

$\frac{4}{4}$ ○• = ○ ♩   **6 beats or counts**

♩• = ♩ ♩   **3 beats or counts**

♩• = ♩ ♪   **1½ beats or counts**

♪• = ♪ ♫   **¾ of one beat or count**

6/8   ♩• = ♪ ♪ ♪   **3 beats or counts**

A DOT EQUALS ONE HALF THE VALUE OF THE NOTE BEFORE THE DOT.

THE METER SIGNATURE

ONE OF THE MAIN CONCEPTS TO UNDERSTAND IS THE MEANING OF THE NUMBERS IN THE METER SIGNATURE.

$$\frac{4}{4} \qquad \frac{3}{4} \qquad \frac{2}{4} \qquad \frac{6}{8} \qquad \frac{9}{8} \qquad \frac{12}{8} \qquad \frac{2}{2} \qquad \frac{5}{4} \qquad \frac{7}{4}$$

THE TOP NUMBER TELLS YOU HOW MANY BEATS THERE ARE IN EACH MEASURE, AND THE BOTTOM NUMBER TELLS YOU WHAT TYPE OF NOTE RECEIVES ONE COUNT.

EXAMPLE:

TOP   4   MEANS THERE ARE FOUR BEATS IN EACH MEASURE
BOTTOM   4   MEANS THAT A QUARTER NOTE RECEIVES ONE COUNT

Top   12   MEANS THERE ARE TWELVE BEATS IN EACH MEASURE
Bottom   8   MEANS THAT AN EIGHTH NOTE RECEIVES ONE BEAT (COUNT)

Top   2   MEANS THERE ARE TWO BEATS IN EACH MEASURE
Bottom   2   MEANS THAT A HALF-NOTE RECEIVES ONE BEAT (COUNT)

Reading and Counting Music Rhythm Patterns   20

ANOTHER CONCEPT TO UNDERSTAND IS THAT WHEN THE NUMBER IN THE BOTTOM HALF OF THE METER SIGNATURE SHOWS A **2**....

EXAMPLE:　　　　　　　　TOP　　**2**
　　　　　　　　　　　　　　BOTTOM　**2**

ALL NOTE VALUES WHILE IN THAT METER SIGNATURE WILL DECREASE IN VALUE BY HALF.

EXAMPLE:

THE VALUE OF THE SAME NOTES IN 4/4 TIME

WHEN THE NUMBER IN THE BOTTOM HALF OF THE METER SIGNATURE SHOWS AN EIGHTH...

EXAMPLE:

Top $\quad$ **6**

Bottom $\quad$ **8**

ALL NOTE VALUES WHILE IN THAT METER SIGNATURE WILL DOUBLE IN VALUE AS COMPARED TO THEIR VALUE IN COMMON TIME OR **4/4**.

EXAMPLE:

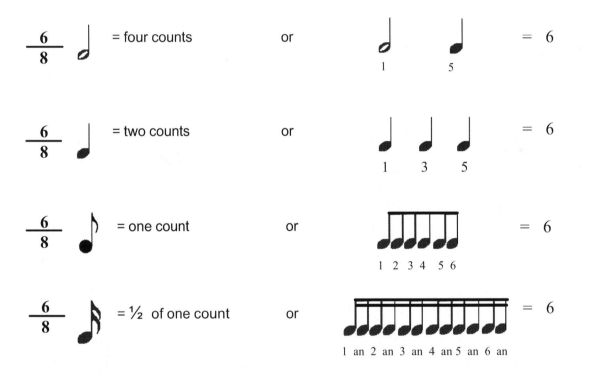

WITH THE UNDERSTANDING OF THESE CONCEPTS, YOU ARE NOW READY TO IMMERSE YOURSELF IN THE COUNTING OF MUSICAL PATTERNS AND DEVELOPING THE FREEDOM TO SIGHTREAD MUSIC.

1. <u>NOTES</u> ARE COUNTED AND SOUNDED, THEREFORE THE NOTES ARE <u>NUMBERED</u>.
   EXAMPLE:

2. <u>RESTS</u> ARE COUNTED BUT NOT SOUNDED, THEREFORE RESTS <u>**ARE NOT**</u> NUM-
BERED.
   EXAMPLE:

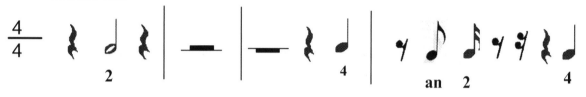

3. A DOT AFTER A NOTE MEANS THAT THE DOT WILL RECEIVE ONE-HALF (½) OF THE
VALUE OF THE NOTE BEFORE THE DOT.
   EXAMPLE:

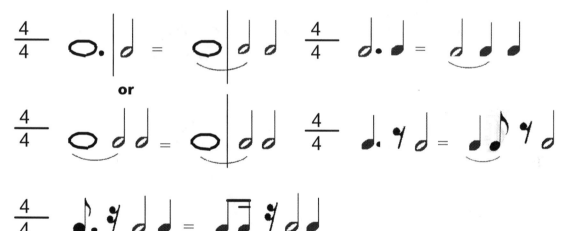

4. WHEN A NOTE IS SUSTAINED FOR MORE THAN ONE COUNT (BEAT), IT IS NUM-
BERED FOR THE COUNT ON WHICH IT IS SOUNDED AND NOT NUMBERED FOR THE
COUNTS ON WHICH THE SOUND IS SUSTAINED (OR HELD).
   EXAMPLE:

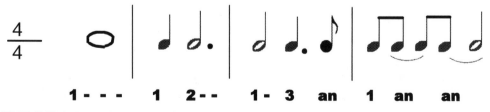

THE REMAINING VALUE OF THE NOTE IS MENTALLY COUNTED, SO THAT ONE KNOWS
PRECISELY AT WHAT TIME TO SOUND THE NEXT NOTE.

5. THE VALUE OF THE REST IS THE SAME VALUE AS A NOTE, THEREFORE, THE REST MUST BE RESPECTED AND RECEIVE ITS FULL VALUE.
   EXAMPLE:

1   2   an 4

3   an an der an

6. The following are examples of note and rest values, and how they should be counted.

Whole note=four counts

1

Whole rest=four counts

Two half notes=four counts

1 — 3 —

Two half rests=four counts

Four quarter notes=four counts

1 2 3 4

Four quarter rests=four counts

Eight eighth notes=four counts

1 an 2 an 3 an 4 an

Eight eighth rests=four counts

Sixteen sixteenth notes=four counts

1 der an dah 2 der an dah 3 der an dah 4 der an dah

Sixteen sixteenth rests=four counts

Four sets of triplets=four counts

1 an dah   2 an dah   3 an dah   4 an dah

Four sets of triplet rests=four counts

Two quarter note triplets=four counts

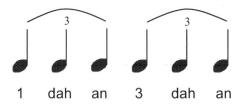

1   dah   an   3   dah   an

Two quarter note triplet rests=four counts

In the example below, we see the relationship between a quarter note triplet and an eighth note triplet and how the counting is derived. In other words, the first two eighth notes of the eighth note triplet represent the first quarter note of the quarter note triplet.

The third note of the first eighth note triplet and the first note of the second eighth note triplet represent the second quarter note of the first quarter note triplet.

The second note of the second eighth note triplet and the third note of the eighth note triplet represent the third quarter note of the first quarter note triplet.

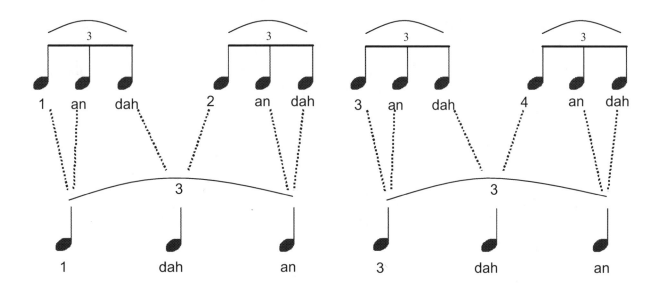

HOW TRIPLETS ARE COUNTED AND WHY

Eighth note triplets are counted…..

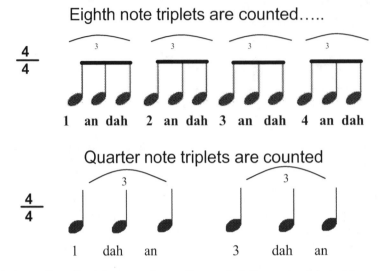

Quarter note triplets are counted

It takes the first two notes of an eighth note triplet to equal the first quarter note of a quarter note triplet.

When the first and second note of the eighth note triplet are tied and the third note of the eighth note triplet is tied to the first note of the second eighth note triplet (see Figure 1, page 27) and the second and third note of the second group of triplets are tied, then we can show the relationship to the quarter note triplet as seen in Figure 2, page 27.

The first note of the third triplet is tied to the second note of the third triplet and the third note of the third triplet is tied to the first note of the fourth triplet and the second note of the fourth triplet is tied to the third note of the fourth triplet. The following count takes place….

Continued on Page 27

Relationship of eighth note triplets to quarter note triplets are shown below.

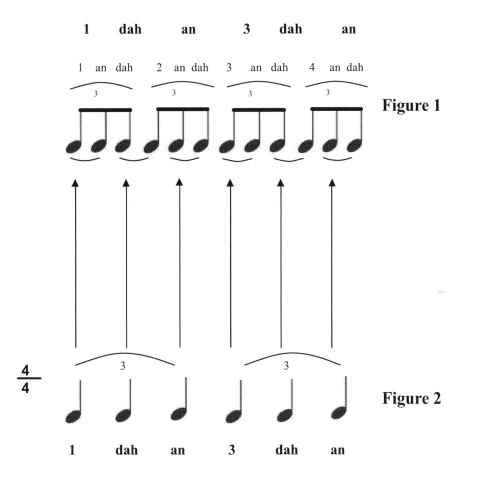

Figure 1

Figure 2

Additional samples of triplet and quarter note triplets can be seen on Page 28.

Continuation of Triplet Examples

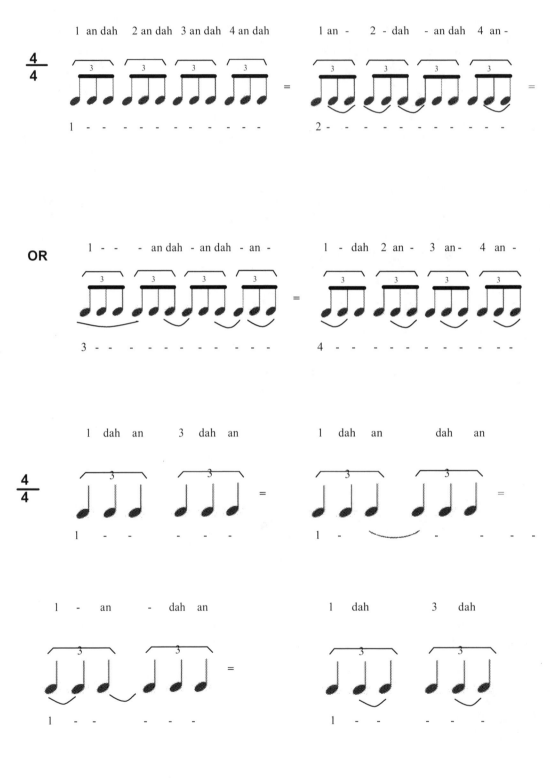

Examples of counting different rhythms as seen, and as counted in 4/4 time.

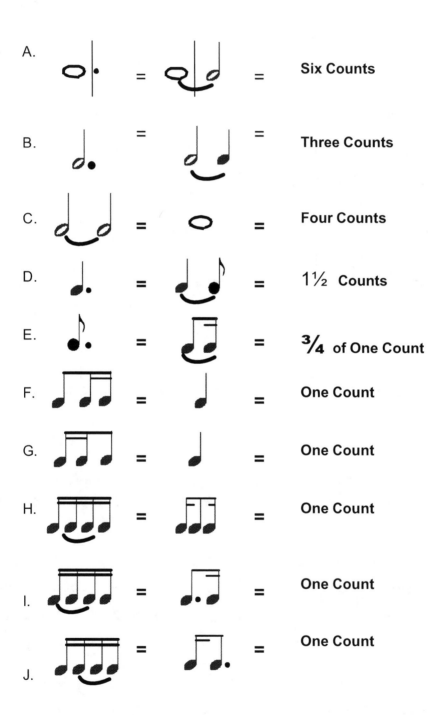

A. = = **Six Counts**

B. = = **Three Counts**

C. = = **Four Counts**

D. = = **1½ Counts**

E. = = **¾ of One Count**

F. = = **One Count**

G. = = **One Count**

H. = = **One Count**

I. = = **One Count**

J. = = **One Count**

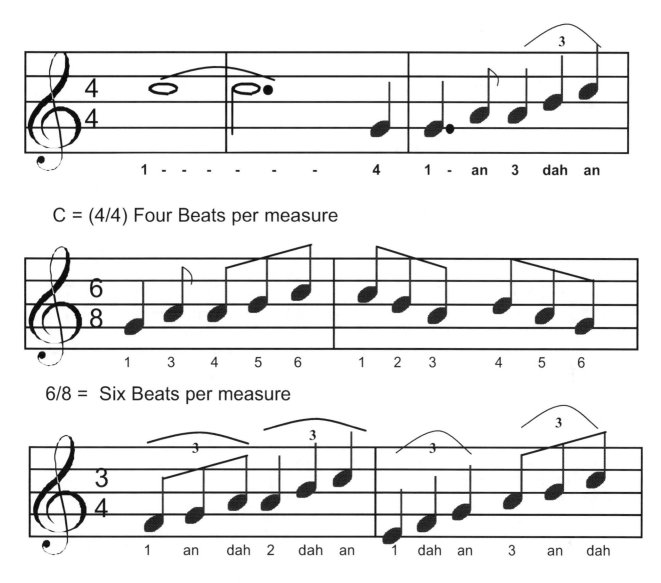

C = (4/4) Four Beats per measure

6/8 = Six Beats per measure

3/4 = Three Beats per measure

If you will use the smallest note value in each measure to work out the note and rest values, each measure becomes easier to count mentally. I strongly recommend that this concept be used in all problem areas. ***Remember to use the slash.***

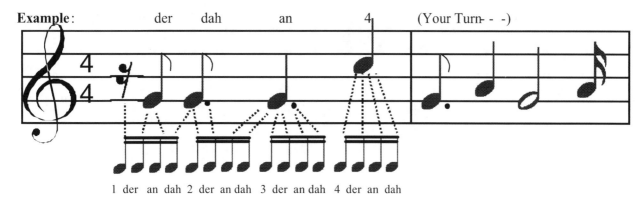

Continued from page 31

Now there is no reason to guess when to play a note or depend on some-one else to know when to play.

EXAMPLE:
&=an

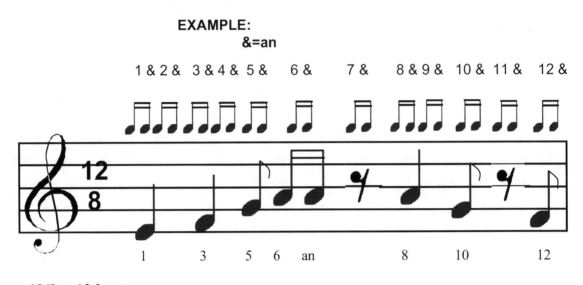

12/8 = 12 beats per measure.

Remember when the meter signature shows an eight at the bottom, each eighth note equals one count, and therefore a sixteenth note receives one-half (½) of one count. In other words, each note doubles in value.
EXAMPLE:

Since my first edition was published, this particular rhythm pattern below was presented in music for a show we were playing and quite a few of the musicians did not know how to count it. I have placed this pattern in this edition for those who may encounter this pattern in the future.

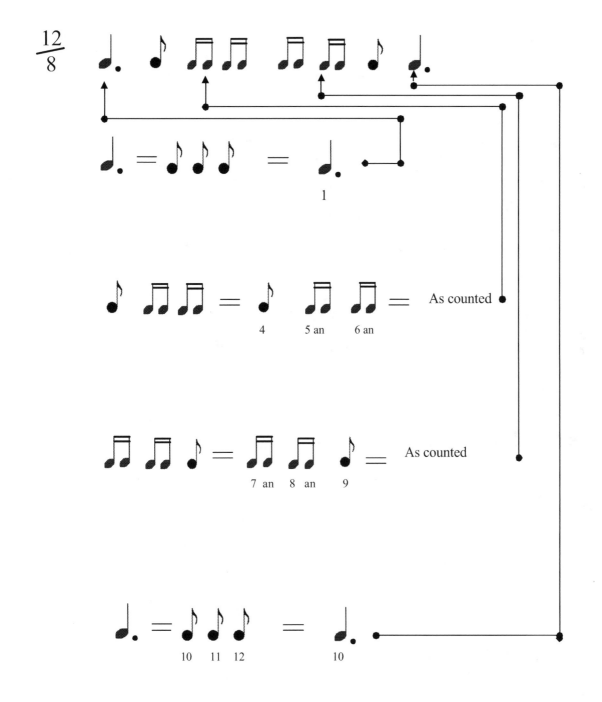

EXERCISES IN COUNTING

Now here are exercises to test your understanding of
these musical concepts. (Exercise 1)

More exercises in Counting (Exercise 2)

Exercise 3

Exercise 4

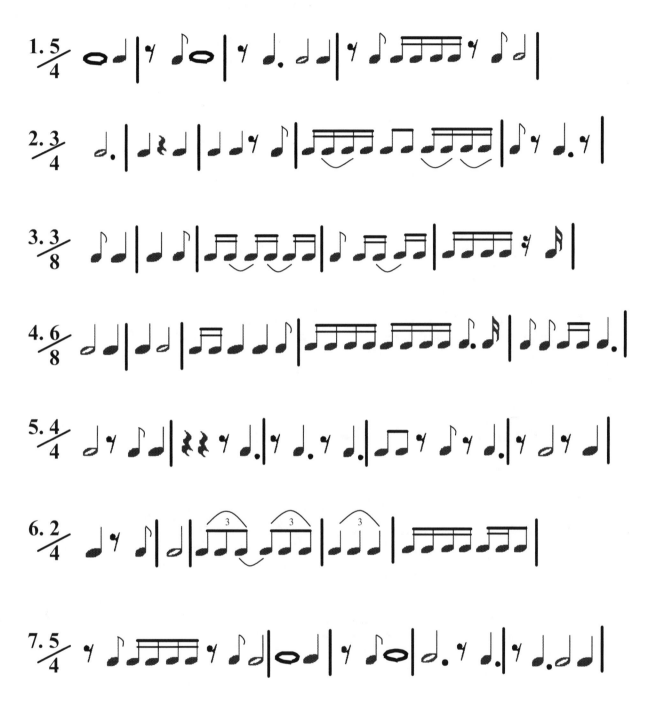

Answers to Page 34 Exercise 1

Answers to Page 35 Exercise 2

Reading and Counting Music Rhythm Patterns

Answers to Page 36 Exercise 3

Answers to Page 37 Exercise 4

Now you are ready to enjoy your music. Don't forget to use the slashes!